ABC WONDERLAND

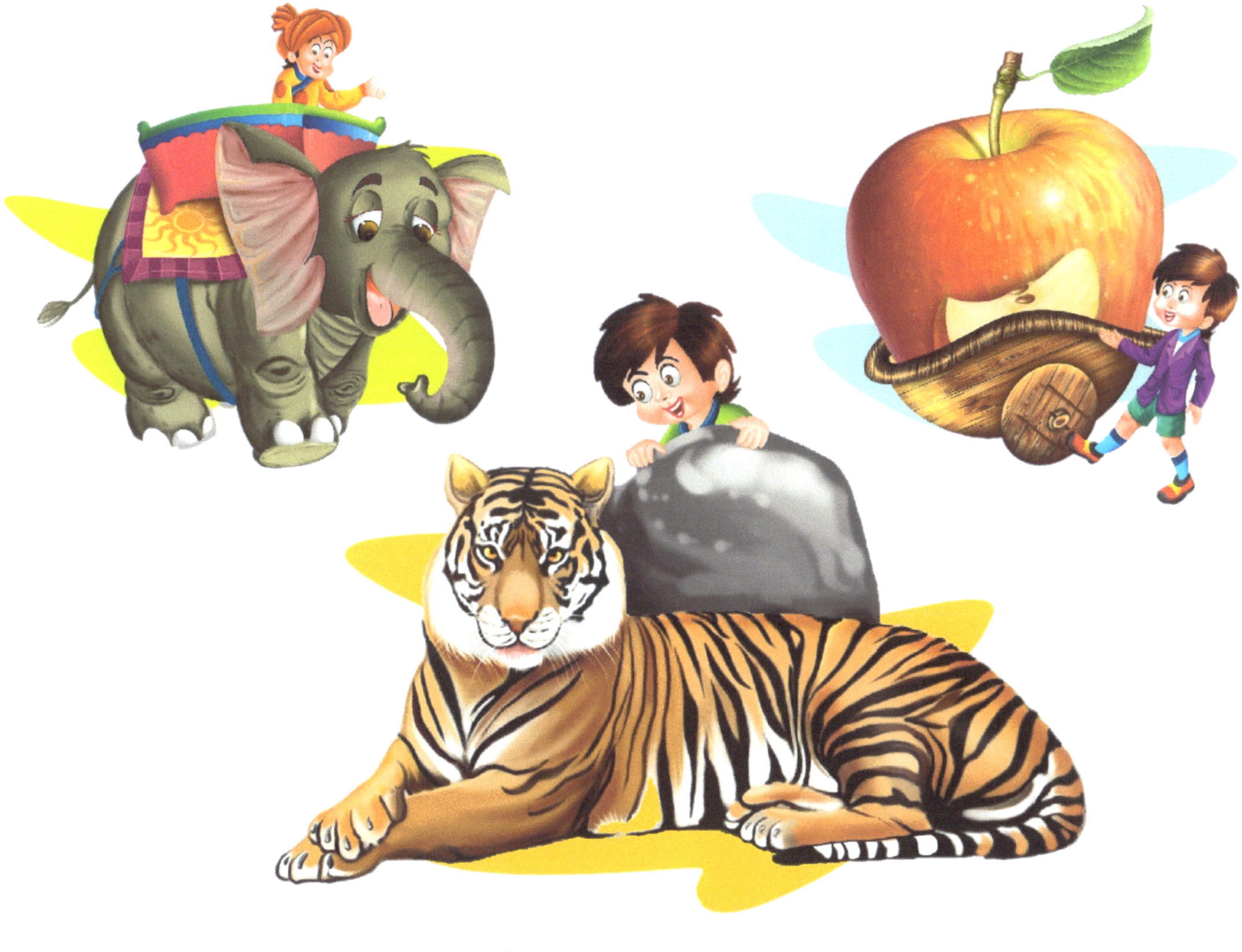

TulsiWonderKids | BY Tulsi Sahitya PUBLICATIONS INDIA

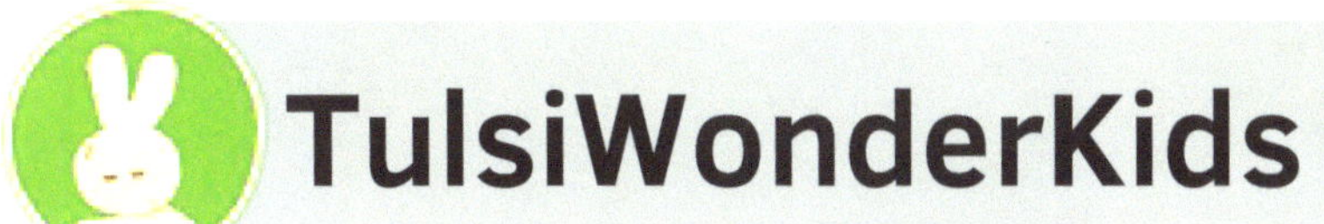

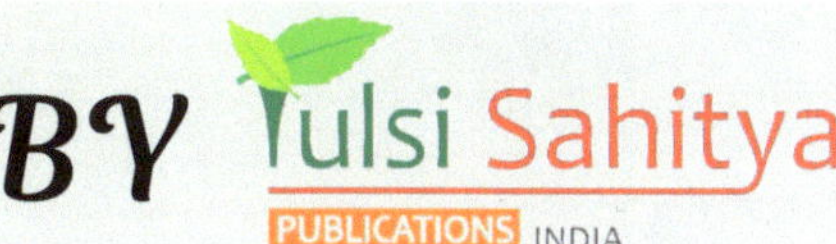

A a

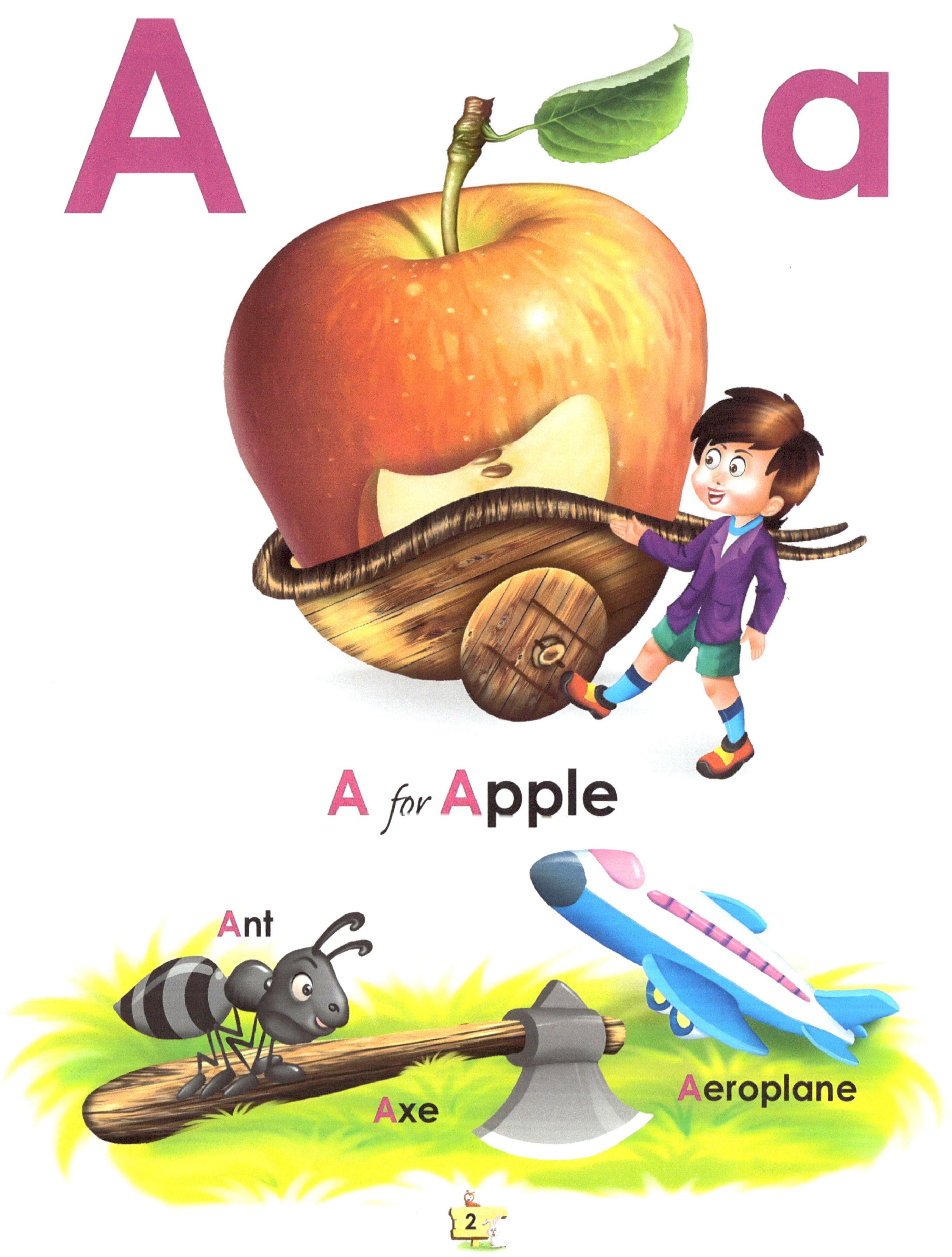

A for **A**pple

Ant

Axe

Aeroplane

B b

B *for* Ball

C c

C *for* Cat

Cow

Cup

Cock

D d

D _for_ **D**og

Drum   **D**ustbin   **D**en

E e

E *for* **E**lephant

Eraser

Egg

Engine

F f

F *for* **F**ish

Five　　　**F**ox　　　**F**lower

G g

G _for_ **Grapes**

Gate　　**G**oat　　**G**irl

H h

H *for* **H**orse

I i

I *for* **I**ce-cream

J j

J *for* **J**ug

Joker

Jeep

Jacket

K k

K *for* **K**ite

Kid

Kettle

Key

L l

L *for* Lion

Leaf

Lamp

Lotus

M m

M for Monkey

Mop

Mat

Mug

N n

N *for* **N**est

Nine   **N**ut   **N**ail

O o

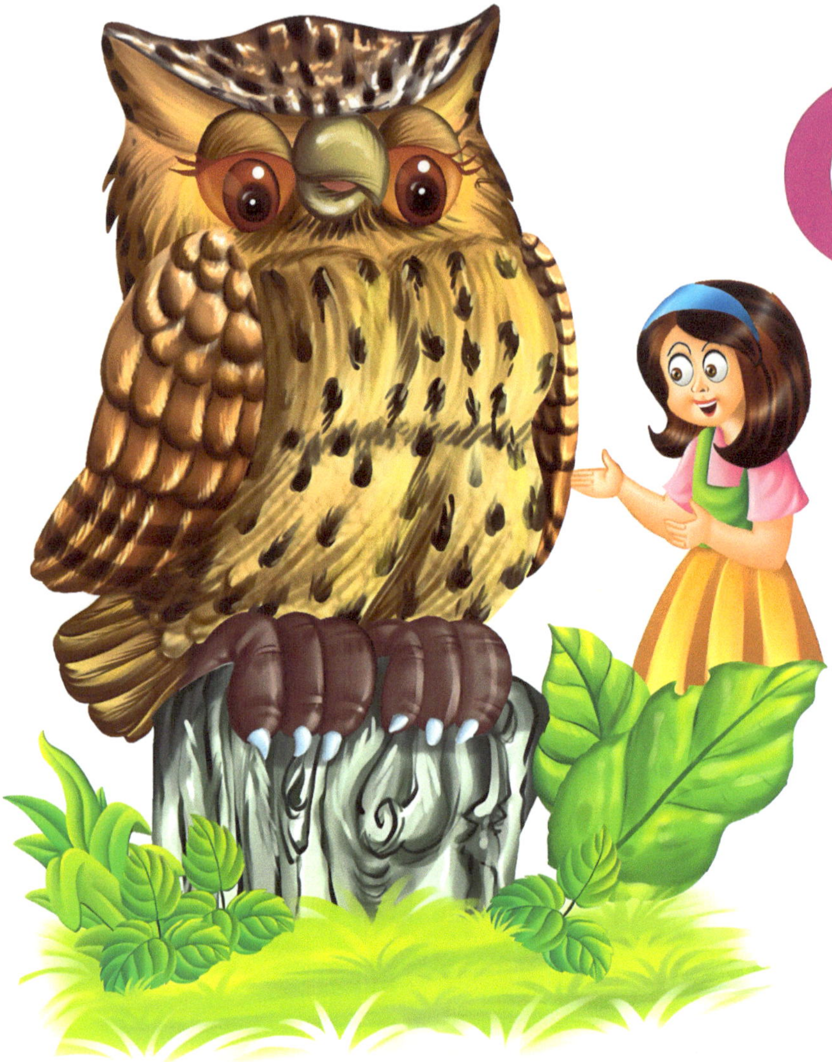

O *for* Owl

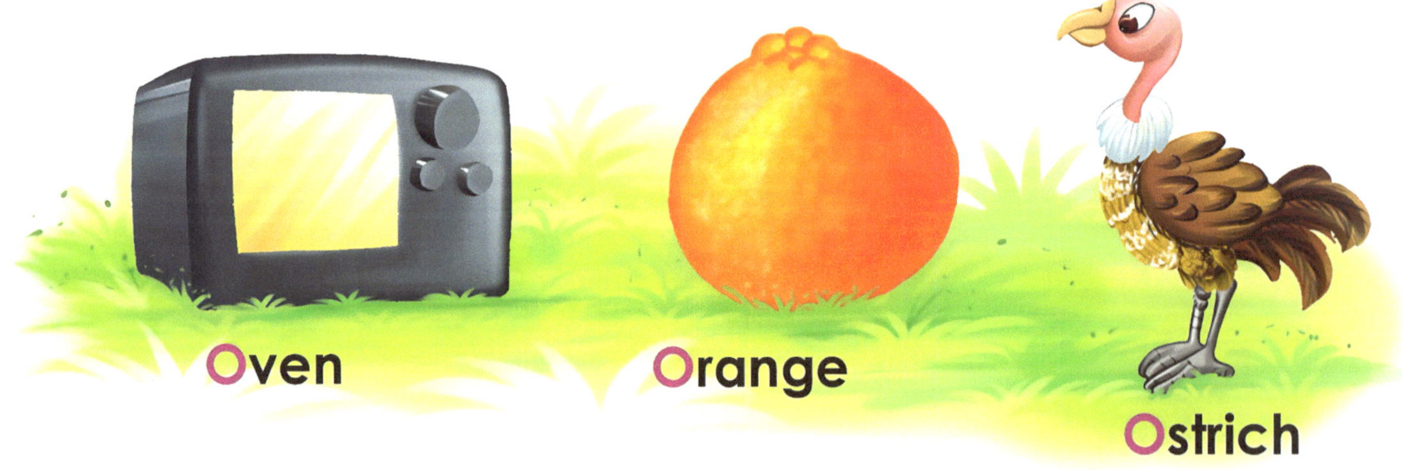

Oven
Orange
Ostrich

P   p

P *for* Parrot

Pineapple

Pear

Pencil

Q q

Q *for* **Q**ueen

Quill

Quail

Question mark

R r

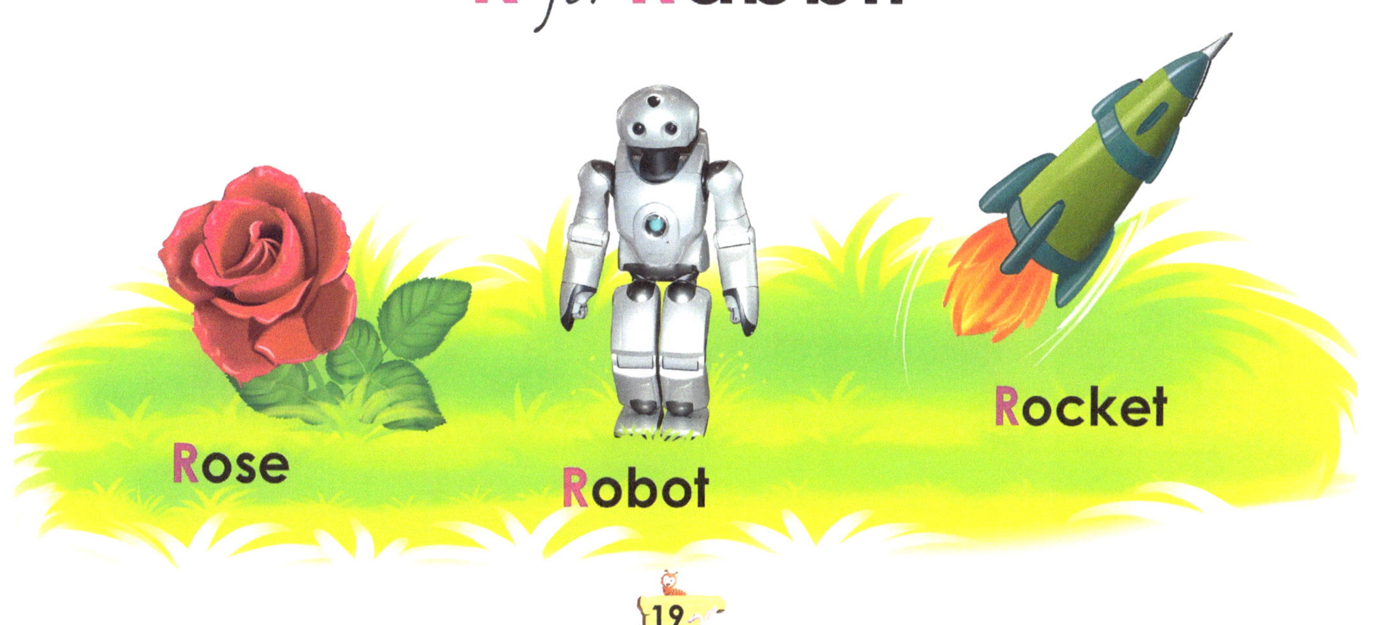

R *for* **R**abbit

Rose

Robot

Rocket

S s

S *for* **S**quirrel

T t

T for **T**iger

U

U

U _for_ **Umbrella**

Urn **U**niform **U**nicorn

V

V

V *for* **V**an

Vulture   **V**est   **V**egetables

W w

W for **W**ell

Wall

Wheel

Watch

X x

X for X-mas tree

X-ray **Xylophone** **Xerox**

Y y

Y *for* **Y**acht

Z z

Z *for* **Z**ebra

Zero   **Z**ip   **Z**ig-Zag

 **Aa**
 **Bb**
 **Cc**
 **Dd**
 **Ee**
 **Ff**

 **Gg**
 **Hh**
 **Ii**
 **Jj**
 **Kk**
 **Ll**

 **Mm**
 **Nn**
 **Oo**
 **Pp**
 **Qq**
 **Rr**

 **Ss**
 **Tt**
 **Uu**
 **Vv**
 **Ww**
 **Xx**

 **Yy**
 **Zz**

Match The Picture With Correct Letter

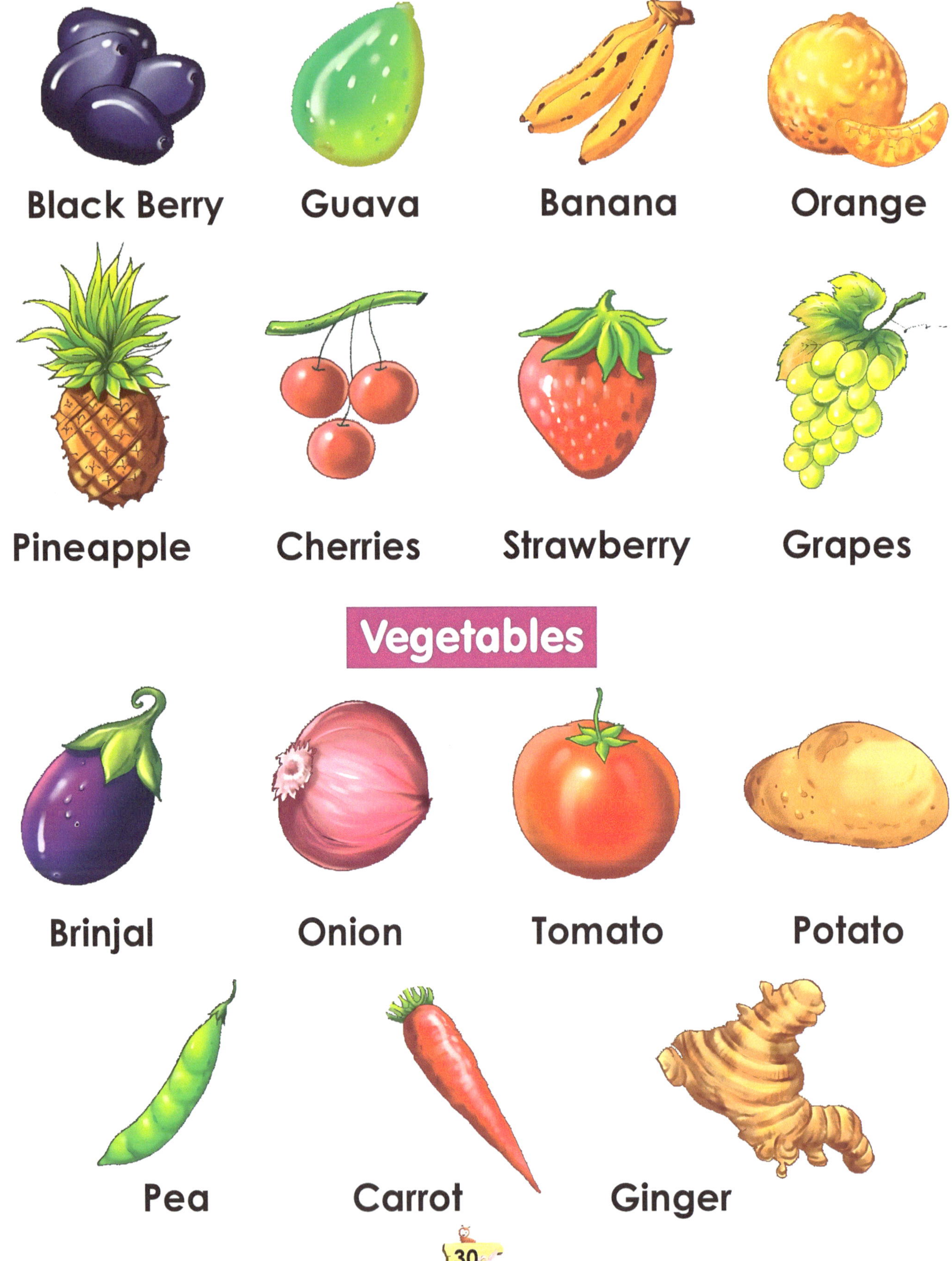

Fruits
Black Berry
Guava
Banana
Orange
Pineapple
Cherries
Strawberry
Grapes
Vegetables
Brinjal
Onion
Tomato
Potato
Pea
Carrot
Ginger

Animals

Birds

Flowers

Colours